INCLINATIONS

by
David B Harrington

April 2011

"Inclinations"
Copyright © 2009 **David B. Harrington**

ISBN: 1-882918-27-4

Page Design by: Lee Klopfer

Cover Design & Creation by: David B. Harrington / Lee Klopfer

Publishing Dreams
www.rev-press.com

This book is dedicated in loving memory of my mother, Julie Gelston Harrington (1919-2005)

Table of Contents

Part 2 cont...

"Book of All Ages"

ANGELIC ORIGIN

In the beginning of time there was only cold, dark, empty space. Therefore God created the stars and called them the heavens, and the cold, dark, empty space was generated with warmth, light and energy.

All of space was without gravity, form or matter and the Spirit of God moved through the heavens.

Amidst the heavens God made the holy angels, and they greatly magnified the Divine Grace of God.

And the Holy Angels of Light were counted with the stars of heaven. And God instructed the holy angels, commanding them to abide by His Will.

And they sang praise to God and worshipped His Throne continually with honor and glory, power and authority.

And God looked down upon the heavens and upon the holy angels that He had made and blessed them all.

ANGELIC REBELLION

In the midst of heaven, round about His mighty Throne, God planted a beautiful rose garden.

But now it seems that Lucifer, whom God had set high above the other holy angels, for his was the most brilliant shining star in all the heavens, grew exceedingly jealous of God and lifted his wings in fury against God's supreme glory.

So enraged with envy, Lucifer gathered together a legion of angels. And they coveted together and conspired to rebel against God's Throne and overthrow heaven.

And they turned away from the Will of God and worshipped Lucifer as God.

Now God had foreknowledge over all things, even from the beginning, and He filled with vengeance.

But Lucifer's heart waxed hot with greedy resentment and he plucked a rose from out of the garden. And he took the rose and fled from the garden, and from the face of God.

So God sought to punish Lucifer, but the wicked angels repelled and defended Lucifer against the holy angels.

And God said unto the wicked angels, "Lucifer has deceived himself, are you going to let him deceive you as well?"

However, God's warning only made the wicked angels all the more angry and war broke out in heaven. Lucifer and the wicked angels fought fiercely against Michael and the holy angels, but prevailed not.

And God took hold of Lucifer and said unto him, "You deceiver of angels, you have forsaken me. Thus I hereby condemn you to eternal corruption for your wickedness."

And the holy angels that joined Lucifer's legion increased greatly in numerous multitudes: For they feared not the angry wrath of God.

So God made more holy angels to replace them.

And He commanded them, and all the holy angels.

Now there were as many roses in the garden as there were stars in the heavens and God blessed each one. And God said unto Lucifer and his band of rebel angels, for there was a great subdivision, "I once called you holy, but now I call you wicked: For you have turned away from my Will to partake in the evildoings of foolish pride.

"And you have deliberately disobeyed my commandments and followed in the footsteps of a bad example set forth to seek after treasures unobtainable.

"You have spoiled what was once holy with your greed, and for you and those that have chosen to partake in your iniquities, I leave no room for repentance.

"Furthermore, as for the rose you have stolen, keep it in remembrance of the evil you have committed here in heaven: For here in heaven you shall no more be welcome. I ask not for it back, but because you have taken a single rose, I shall curse every seed that springs up to flower in the garden, beginning with yours, henceforth throughout all eternity.

LUCIFERIC DESCENT

Knowing their fate of doom, the wicked angels one by one plucked their roses from the garden.

And God took hold of Lucifer and bound him. And he clipped Lucifer's wings and cast him from heaven, and his rose. And this did God do the same to all the wicked angels, one by one, beginning with Lucifer.

And the stars that had been counted with Lucifer and the wicked angels God did cause to fall. And as old stars would die, new ones were born.

And the stars that remained shining in heaven was three time as many angels that had fallen from grace.

Afterward God planted a new rose garden to replace the old. The number of roses in the new garden was three times as many as were in the old and God blessed each one with thorns.

So God dispirited Lucifer and the wicked angels and took away from them their divine nature. And He flung them down from heaven into the bowels of the newly formed earth and forbid them never to return.

Part 1

LIVING BUTTERFLIES

In the season of wither when all that is living falls to the earth and dies, the Almighty Word of God went out to Tixen in the wilderness countryside and was spoken by his angel saying, "Breathe in with a deep breath."

And when Tixen had done what the angel instructed, he then said unto him, "Now let loose your breath out over the face of the earth." And when I did, there straightaway blew a mighty strong gale over the face of the earth, insomuch that the trees from the North to the South and from the East to the West were heavily shaken.

And I looked, and behold, the leaves off the trees were turned into beautiful Living Butterflies: So wonderful to gaze upon and of many fantastic colors and I was bewildered at their beauty.

But the angel turned quickly and rebuked me saying, "Be not deceived such as the ungodly of the earth are, as you shall now see." And I looked and saw the ungodly of the earth, who were made gay by reason of the splendid colors of the butterflies. Yet were blinded by their hallucinations and thought themselves to be in paradise, but were deceived. And they commenced to sing and dance around merrily in circles, engaging in all manners of lust and fornication. And were made exuberant because of their drunkenness.

And I heard the angel again say to me, "Breathe in with a deep breath." And immediately the winds ceased and the leaves were no more shaken from the trees. And those that turned into Living Butterflies fell to the ground and choked in the burning heat of the sun. And I saw the ungodly of the earth who were buried up to their necks. And many therefore starved to death because they could not find a place to prepare their meats.

And I heard the angel declare with a loud voice, "Let the ungodly of the earth remain always so: For they are fools to believe that the Lord would spare them unless they repent of their deeds. Or to think that they should be found worthy to come into heavenly places by way of their ungodliness.

"But rather, because they are blinded by the bright colors of the butterflies, which are now brown and decayed, and driven by their lewd desires, and of their exceeding drunkenness, shall scorn with hatred the Lord God their Creator evermore. And be cast into hell and tormented with fire, save a few who shall quickly repent of their adulteries, whom of which I shall show you afterward."

After this there came up from out of the earth and from out of the caves armies of winged rodents. And scurrying about with razor-sharp teeth, they began feeding on the rotting meats that the ungodly of the earth had left behind. And they became infected with many horrible diseases and driven into a mad frenzy. And they began to eat the flesh of the ungodly, both living and dead, and many more were made sick and died.

But the rest cried out with a loud voice saying, "Lord God, have pity on our wretched souls!" And as many who were found worthy were saved.

And I heard a voice like a thousand rustling winds answer and say, "Not so: For the ungodly of the earth shall not confess of their sins. Neither shall they give glory to God or submit to His Will."

And I heard the angel say unto me, "Now let loose your breath out over the face of the earth." And when I did, half of heaven and half of earth were filled with a foul stench: So wretched and so vile was this stench that even more became nauseous and gagged to their end.

And I , too, would have fainted when I heard the angel answer and say, "Arise and stand tall, O you servant of Christ: Have faith in God and no harm shall befall you." And looking around I saw that the plague of winged rodents the Lord had sent to infest the earth had passed away. Neither was I affected of that foul stench which the Lord God had brought down as punishment against the ungodly of the earth.

And I rejoiced with exceeding gladness because of it. And falling on my face in gratitude, thanked the Lord God Almighty.

FIRST MAN & WOMAN

And setting my eyes to the East, I saw, as it were, the First Man and Woman in the midst of paradise, whom remained pure and undefiled, walking upright and justly in the Commandments of God. And they were attended continually by hosts of heavenly angels.

And I heard incessant voices like chanting and glorious praises coming forth from out of the Holy Mountain: Turning to see, I saw five ancient men in long white robes bowing before an Altar of Fire. And they had each one of them a hood covering their heads and long white beards: For they are God's hermits, strong in faith, devout men of great holiness, with the wisdom and knowledge of the ages.

And it was instructed of them that they should offer up continuous prayers for the protection of the First Man and Woman, and for the Book, which had withstood the sands of time and was preserved; and to guard it from the greedy clutches of the serpent.

And on the right side of the Altar of Fire I saw an open tabernacle. And from out of it proceeded lightning.

And one of the ancients beckoned me and said, "Come

closer." And when I did, I saw the First Man and Woman approach the Altar of Fire, as would a bride and her groom.

And in her hands I saw the Book rolled up like a scroll and sealed up in a golden cylinder. And she brought it forth and deposited it into the Tabernacle of God: For it was found holy.

And immediately the tabernacle was shut up tight. And I heard the five ancients give glory to God saying, "Lord God, You are rich in power and might and righteous in all your Judgments. Even the holy angels are numbered in ranks. But You, Lord God, are Justice Supreme!"

After this I saw the First Man and Woman standing blameless and triumphant before the Altar of Fire. And in his hand he bore a new book rolled up like a scroll and sealed with three strong seals.

And I heard the five ancients fall on their faces in a victorious praise. And all of heaven was shaken. And there was thunder and I heard many voices that uttered forth from out of the clouds and from out of God's Throne proclaiming, "Behold O heaven and earth:
For the Great Judgment of thine accuser the serpent is come!"

And it was made known unto me of their great accomplishments in overcoming the serpent through many hardships and tribulations.

And one of the ancients said unto me, "What you see write in a book and seal it up:
For it, too, shall be retained as Judgment against the serpent in the end times."

- Judgment Seals -
FALL OF SAINT MICHAEL'S

After seven years and seven months and seven days that colossal Cathedral of Saint Michael's was built. And I saw the pilgrims of faith flocking by the thousands to that Holy City which deceives the whole world with its greed and with its power and with its wealth.

From out of every nation they were called. By land and by sea and by air they came forth to worship and to celebrate in its splendor.

And they joined together in prayer along with their king and all his bishops and cardinals, and with all their scholars, until the Holy City swelled with the sound of their vain repetitions.

And God was angered, and all of heaven with Him. And I heard a loud voice say, "Woe unto the so-called well learned leaders of faith, who call themselves apostles and ministers of God, and are not. But do lie and deceive the people and drag my children away from the truth. And brainwash them, making them to believe in their false doctrines and twisted dogmas, with faith borne out of ignorance and fear. Woe unto you, O cursed impostors, for you shall receive your rewards!"

And I looked and saw that mighty mountain Vesuvius bellow to life and erupt with vengeance. And there was a great earthquake, fire and brimstone.

And after three days and three nights that colossal Cathedral of Saint Michael's came toppling to the ground. And many pilgrims of faith and innocent people were crushed under its enormous weight.

And no more were the sounds of pipes or bells heard in the Holy City. And I watched in horror as the people were sent running and screaming into the streets And I was stunned and amazed, for that Holy City which deceives the whole world was left in shambles.

And I was angered at God for all the widespread destruction He had wrought upon the Holy City. And I heard a voice from heaven like thunder answer and say, "You are angry with me because of my great wrath?"

And I shuddered with exceeding fear and answered, "What's need be, O Lord, according to Your Will." But from this time on I abstained anymore from questioning the Lord about His Judgments.

GOSPEL PREACHING GYPSIES

And when he had broken open the second Judgment Seal, I saw tens of thousands of gypsy caravans migrating out of the West. And they went about in bands, traveling from town to town and village to village preaching the Holy Gospel of Jesus saying, "You are not unlike that old fox Herod murdering innocent children as you do."

And they preached with fiery tongues in this manner, upholding strong opposition against the murdering of unborn children saying, "The Lord of heaven and earth is wroth because what He has created and blessed with His own hands you put asunder and destroy with your wicked designs. Therefore, repent quickly or else Great Judgment will befall you all!

"Even the Queen of Angels, that lovely and divine Empress of Heaven, has she not visited all your countries and appeared unto all your children?"

But the people soon grew sick and tired of the gypsies and plotted to do away with them once and for all. And I saw them gather by the multitudes at that sacred shrine where they venerate the martyrs and encompass the gypsys' camp.

Then at nightfall I watched them descend upon the gypsies like bloodhounds, who were breaking bread and sipping wine, and had formerly given up many of their old customs and superstitions and kept the Commandments of Christ. And many cast their silver and gold and precious jewels into the fire as a testimony against the people's sins: For the Spirit of the Lord was upon them all and they were filled with the Holy Ghost.

So they sent scouts up ahead to meet with the leaders of the people to try and settle their indifferences saying, "The sins of the world are raging like a fire on high! 'But vengeance is mine', saith the Lord."

But the people were outraged with the gypsies and stoned the scouts to death. And they stormed the shrine with whips and torches and went rampaging throughout the gypsys' camp, setting their tents ablaze, overturning wagons, desecrating the Host and killing mercilessly.

And I watched in sheer horror as young gypsy maidens were brutally violated by the hundreds. And many were bound and dragged away captive into that great city whose church shall be destroyed by the invading army from the West.

And they were tortured with fire and cast like vagrants into prison to die. And some managed to escape and fled into the hills. But the rest were roasted like pigs over beds of hot burning coals.

And the Lord was furious with the people. And there proceeded fire down from heaven and devoured them up.

AGENTS OF HELL

After these things were finished, I saw the Agents of Hell disguised as little children and as apostles that were set loose upon the world. And they went about from door to door like packs of ravenous wolves devouring up the little children.

And up from out of the pit there crept foul spirits like snakes, whose number is unto all of man's vain superstitions: The spirits of devils working great miracles inso to pit man against man and against his God. The spirits of demons and graven images, idols and false gods unforgotten, whom every nation has worshipped and served since the beginning of the world. And have caused countless denominations, indifferences and divisions among the people.

And having great wings like dragons, these dreadful spirit creatures followed them like shadows into every house. And the very Altar of God was corrupted because of them.

But behold! Down from the Holy Mountain there came a glorious sight: Dragonslayers accompanied with the angels of heaven. Mighty warriors of great strength and valor.

Now to each one was given a sharp lance and shields bearing the Holy Cross of Jesus. And they were commanded by God to slay the dragons that had laid hold of the earth.

And looking up to the heavens, I saw two mighty angels holding up the Big and Little Dippers. And when the Word was given, one of the angels tipped the Big Dipper and out poured hot oils over the multitudes. And many were scalded to death because of this terrible plague. And I was sore afraid because of it.

   Then when the Word was given, the other angel tipped the Little Dipper and there was a spectacular miracle: A magnificent star fell to the earth and the remainder of the wicked vanished away with their offspring. And the name of this magnificent star is called: "HONEYWINE"

Part 2

TWO RAMS

Come: Look and see the wonderful sights through the eyes of the visionary.

I was driven by the Spirit to a high plateau near a river of rushing waters. And overlooking the sea wall where the waters cascade into the sea, stood two, like rams, clothed in long flowing robes all decked in gold.

And in their hands I saw them juggling open books as would a pair of charlatans. And out of the mouth of one I saw fabulous tongues of fire stretch forth over the congregation. And in the eyes of the other welled up great pools of water that whenever he opened his mouth to speak, an endless flood of tears would pour down upon the congregation: In order to extinguish the flames that the first ram had spit forth from out of his mouth.

Above the crashing of the waves I could hear the rams speaking great things concerning the Living God before the assembly, who had come to witness the powers of their healing word. But when they spoke their words clashed and went against one another, not too far between.

Nevertheless, the rams stood fearlessly in the midst of the congregation, facing each other in bitter opposition, kicking and snorting as they prepared to do battle. And bowing their heads in prayer, they charged at full throttle.

And when the rams locked horns, I heard a loud crack of thunder. And all about the arena the mountain rattled. And it was high tide and the waves were battering ferociously against the sea wall. And the boulders were loosened from their places, and the great slabs of marble, granite and slate of their temples broke loose from their foundation and washed out to sea.

And their faith faltered and gave out from under them
by way of their pride and shame. And their ministries fell
hard against the rocks and broke apart. And their lavish
kingdoms were thrown down hard with mighty vengeance
against the sea wall and crumbled to pieces.

And the congregation disputed one with the other over
the great things which the rams had spoken in their midst:
For one spoke vehemently and with great authority, and
the other mildly. And the assembly was torn in two and
divided by way of the great things which the rams had
spoken. And departing from the midst, went their separate
ways.

And as I stood wondering what these things might mean, I
heard the angel answer and say,
"Marvel not: For I shall show you the cause of the rams'
great downfall, with whom they have committed adultery."

And as the angel was yet speaking, behold, up from out
of the midst of the congregation arose a she-goat despoiled
with the filth of the earth. And she ascended to the crest of
the mountain and opened her mouth to speak great things
against the rams.

And the she-goat had a small following that went up after
her with hammers and chisels that they might carve in
stone every glorious word that proceeded out of her mouth.
And she lashed out fearlessly against the rams, accusing
them of debauchery and treachery. And the congregation
was appalled at the rams and cast them into prison because
of the glorious words which the she-goat had spoken.

290 DAYS

Come and see the terrible sights through the eyes of the visionary.

It was Fall Equinox and I was headed for lower ground when looking up, I saw a great gull circling above. And leading me down the face of the mountain, I was drawn like a magnet to the sea. And being about the second hour of the day, I could hear the surf pounding gently against the rocks as I stood by the water's edge with my feet planted firmly in the sand.

Clutched tightly in the gull's beak I saw a long rope with both its ends dangling in space. And a full moon rose in the Eastern sky above the ocean. And I watched in fascination as an angel took up one end of the rope and looped it around the moon like a noose. And with the other end of the rope still grasped snugly in her bill, the gull soared across the horizon. And flew straight into the sun with the moon towing behind her.

And I watched as the sun was swallowed up by the moon. And the earth was plummeted into total darkness seven minutes. And the stars and planets appeared aligned in a bizarre configuration.

And up from out of the waves came millions of giant salamanders. One by one they crawled until the beach was covered in slime.

And looking up, I again saw the sea gull fly across the horizon tugging the moon behind her. And as the veil of darkness lifted and daylight returned to the earth, I saw the giant amphibians that were caught by the mighty undertow and dragged back out to sea.

Time was virtually swept away as the days, months and years were shortened. There were no more seasons and Dusk and Dawn could not be found. And those grand monuments and towering pillars of stone that the ancient astrologers built came crashing to the ground, one great column upon another. And I saw those who stood by with their sundials fall backward on their heels and flee.

And those that navigate the high seas with compasses and chart their destiny by the stars were blown off course and vanished along with their ships. And all about the face of the deep magnetic storms raged and many more were lost at sea and perished.

And the rotation of the earth was quickened. And the windmills and water wheels of the world were hurled into orbit like spinning tops. And the tides roared furiously as the lunar cycles grew more frequent and the gravitational pull of the moon increased in strength. And I saw those mammoths of the deep that were driven ashore by the hundreds and crushed themselves to death.

Falling flat on my face in the sand, I prayed to God that in His mercy He might spare His servant from harm. And I heard the angel answer and say, "Fear not: For one cycle has passed and a new one is begun! From here on in each year shall consist of two hundred and ninety days. Each month twenty-four days, and each day twenty-one hours. Night and day shall be equally divided in that there will be ten and a half hours of darkness and ten and a half hours of daylight."

And when I had picked myself up, I peered into heaven as would one looking through a seven-dimensional kaleidoscope, and lo and behold, above the wind and weathering there appeared a dazzling phenomena in space: A blazing disk of fire spiraling toward the earth like an enormous dial.

And I saw seven spectacular points of light like the colors of the rainbow shooting forth from out of the wheel like flaming arrows. And upon each of these mysterious crowns were written in glory the seven virtues of faith which come down freely from God to a troubled world.

GREAT MOTHER

Disregard the Great Mother and she'll disregard you when it comes time to suckle her breasts. You who hover above her while your bones turn to dust in her belly, have you forgotten her as well? Do her loving arms fasten you down as you wander aimlessly in the Land of Shadow longing to be free, where nobody has substance and nothing to sustain them but gravity itself.

Remember then, the softness of your Mother's warm caress when she nestled you close to her bosom and brushed gently against your cheek. Remember how you once slumbered peacefully in her womb and dreamt of a hopeful renewal? Remember, as you lie paralyzed in the stench of her bowels, the richness of her beauty and the fragrance of her flowery folds: The sweet aroma of roses and cherry blossoms, laced with lilac.

So come all you blood drinkers and flesh-eaters to the Banquet of the Great Mother! Watch how she trembles and shakes as you cut her to pieces and gnaw at her flesh. Then burn her with fire and laugh in her face, leaving her to smolder in ash.

Feel her icy breath upon you like a cold winter frost, O you who strip away her dignity and rip apart her veil: For even now her sorrows are mounting. Go ahead: Bind her wrists, chain her ankles. Poke her with needles and stick her with pins! But beware children, it is because of you that our Mother is enraged.

She is as wroth as a cosmic dragon: Feel her fiery breath upon you like a hot desert storm. Her lungs are clogged with thick black smoke that fumes from her nostrils, rising up to overwhelm her. The four winds swirl around her, one for every season. Can you hear them whisper her name?

So go ahead: Plant your orchards and vineyards while her skin is still moist, O you who blind her eyes and leave her naked and shivering in the sun to die: For even now her tear drops are falling.

Behold your Mother's glory and kiss her on the cheek. Lift the burden which weighs so heavy on her weary shoulders. She was once a lovely young celestial virgin, pure and unspoiled, in a garden paradise bursting with ripened fruit, sweet and delicious. But how we ravish her like wild animals, who can blame her for rebelling? How much more can she withstand, this Mother of ours, whom we cast aside like a used up whore, all trampled and torn.

Has she not sung us tender lullabies and rocked us gently to sleep in cradles of swan feathers and pine needles? Be kind to your Mother and treat her with respect, I tell you! Why must you thrust her full of holes? Just how much venom must you sink into her veins before she becomes immune and rises up to swallow us like a viper?

Step out into the light, O you Children of Darkness, and cover your eyes with coal. Step out of the darkness, all you Children of Light, with your lamps trimmed way down low. See how your Mother feeds the beasts of the field and the creatures of the forest that assemble at her feet, some by day some by night. The lion, jackal and wildebeest come from miles around just to drink out of her hands and taste her crystal clear waters. The birds of the air nestle in her hair and the fish course through her veins to and fro the heart of her ocean.

Call to mind how she once flowed with milk and honey, and with wine. And now, even in her old age, she is pleased to nourish us with all the essentials of life. What is it that is wrong with us? Are we no better than the hounds and vultures who will be left to lick at her wounds and lap up her blood, or will we rescue in time to save ourselves? I think not.

TINY SEED

After this I found myself standing in the garden of God, when looking up, I saw the clouds part and the sun break through an opening in the sky. And there appeared the angel down from heaven, carried by the rays of the sun.

And he stood beside me in all his glory, his eyes flashing like beacons in the night. And he opened his mouth to speak saying, "Don't be afraid: For I have come here to present you with this token from God."

And holding out my hand, he presented me with a Tiny Seed. And looking down at it, I said, "What is it that God would have me do...and what good can possibly come from such a Tiny Seed?"

But the angel perceiving my thoughts answered, "Simply plant it in the midst of God's garden and see." And when I did, behold, up sprung a tree in the midst of God's garden, shining forth with glory from top to bottom.

And darting in and out of the branches of this wondrous tree were seven pairs of songbirds singing a pretty melody. And all throughout the garden I could hear the voices of the seven archangels, and the voices of those who assemble at God's Throne to worship Him with music and prayer, with instruments crafted from the finest gold, brass and wood to enhance their song.

Encircling the trunk of this wondrous tree I saw a marvelous sight: Seven glowing balls suspended above the ground like tiny planets revolving around an invisible sun. And these magnificent spheres were about the size of a man's fist, each one the color of a polished gemstone.

And dangling from the limbs of this wondrous tree I saw another marvelous sight: The seven virtuous fruits of the Spirit of God, which give new promise and hope to those who delight in the Seven Virtues of Faith.

And over beyond this wondrous tree which grows in the

midst of God's garden, I saw a beautiful brook flowing down from God's Throne like a pure sparkling waterfall, nourishing its roots and replenishing the fruits year round, inso that whosoever should eat of the tree and drink its crystal clear waters, may be blessed with the gift of eternal life.

SERPENT'S JUDGMENT

After this I turned my eyes Eastward, and behold, standing hand in hand high upon the Pentacle of God were the First Man and Woman bathed in the most beautiful white light I have ever seen.

And I was startled by a dreadful hissing noise coming from behind me: Turning to see, I saw the serpent slithering in the grass of God's garden. And he slipped up through the vines to the top of the archway and hid himself among the creeping roses.

But when he became entangled in the thorns and couldn't get free, he looked up to heaven and shook his tail in defiance. And when the serpent saw that he had been cast out of God's garden, he was vexed and went out to seek revenge upon the First Man and Woman.

And gathering up all his satanic forces, the next thing which I heard was the sound of many horsemen thundering off into battle. And from out of the four corners of the world I saw seven evil spirits, like ravens, leading the serpent's forces across the great expanse.

But when the serpent saw the rings of fire encircling the Holy Mountain, he swelled with bitter contempt. And wrapping his pristine body around the circumference of the earth, he began to squeeze like a giant constrictor in a futile attempt to extract the dragon's rose, which had been placed in a perpetual state of purity to preserve its original form of beauty.

And I saw two mighty angels come down out of heaven with great chains of darkness and station themselves on the North and South Poles. Then when the Word was given, I watched them swoop down and seize the serpent by the throat and drag him off to the Holy Mountain where the First Man and Woman stood waiting.

And laying him at their feet, I saw the man wield his sword. And with a powerful stroke of Divine Justice, he sliced out the serpent's blasphemous tongue. And the angels took the writhing serpent and cast him into the Altar of Fire to burn forever and ever.

And when they did, I heard those familiar voices in heaven and earth rejoice in a victory song. And I saw a parade of people from every nation under the sun marching around God's garden in a victory celebration. And everywhere were the festive sounds of laughter, cheering, trumpeters and glorious praises. And there were many thunderings, lightning, fireworks and a magnificent double rainbow.

And I beheld as a miraculous shower of rose petals and angel feathers began falling from the sky like snowflakes. And I saw smoke from a golden censer rise from the Holy Mountain and ascend up to God's Throne. And all around me were the sweet smells of jasmine, peppermint, ginger, cinnamon, vanilla, almond, licorice, rose blossoms and other fragrant spices.

And looking up to heaven, behold! I saw the First Man and Woman enthroned in glory, arrayed all in white with scepters in their hands and golden crowns upon their heads, like a King and Queen ready to inherit their most treasured reward.

KEY TO CREATION

Light is the first essence of creation - And with light comes the passing of time.

Gravity is the second essence of creation - And with gravity the movement of Spirit.

Form is the third essence of creation - And with form comes the passing of shadows: The Seven Builders of the Universe who carve out the rocks, forge the mountains and lay the foundation of the earth.

Fire is the first force of nature - And with fire the spark of electrical energy: The Seven Creative Powers of God which awaken the sleeping giants and ignite the skies with glory.

Wind is the third force of nature of nature - And with wind chaos and turbulence over the face of the deep: The Seven Breaths of God who fan the flaming seas with vaporous mists.

Matter is the fourth essence of creation - And with matter evolved the first waters of life, like spawning frogs: The Seven Divine Reflections of God who gently stir the waters like ripples spreading endlessly across a circular sea.

Instinct is the first principle of life - And with instinct, wisdom and knowledge, intelligence and the awareness of a Supreme Being.

Corruption is the last principle of life - And with corruption the passing of life unto death.

SUNGODDESS

After this the angel of the Lord took me up above the clouds and showed me a beautiful lady who stood dazzling as bright as the sun.

And looking down over the earth, I must have seen about a million nomads gathered in the desert watching and praying for a sign in heaven to appear.

Now the beautiful lady went down upon a cloud and stood before the multitudes in the image of the Sungoddess which they had erected in her honor. And they knew it not, but it was made known unto me. And when they saw that the statue had come to life and was shining like the sun, they clutched their beads and dropped to their knees in ecstasy.

And the beautiful lady wept as she talked to the sun worshippers about her many sorrows. But the sun worshippers were weary from their journey across the desert, and were many days without food or water. And when they saw the crimson tear drops trickling down her cheeks and the swords piercing her bleeding heart like a pin cushion, they were struck with grief and hid their heads in the sand.

And the beautiful lady was moved with compassion and sent forth a stream of water to come bubbling up through the rocks.

And I saw those who were sick, lame and blind being led away to be healed.

And she cleansed them all with her miraculous waters and cured them of their diseases.

And from this day on many people turned back to God and were converted.

And bowing in adoration before the image of the Great Sungoddess, they began throwing wild roses at her feet.

And the beautiful lady was very pleased with the sun

worshippers and smiled down upon them like a desert flower.

And when she spread her wings, the sun suddenly started whirling above their heads. And its brilliant rays of light caught the hem of her robe and mantle, turning them from blue to silver, from white to transparent and back again. And her crown of stars sparkled like diamonds in the shimmering light as it twirled around her head like a banded halo.

Then, as the sun worshippers all stood watching in a daze, behold, I saw the sun dance across the sky as it reeled up and down like a giant yo-yo.

DRAGON'S JUDGMENT

After this I was caught up in the Spirit to that place which lies between corruptibility and incorruptibility, when suddenly a blinding light knocked me off my feet dizzy.

And when I opened my eyes, I glimpsed up to Seventh Heaven and saw the Most Ancient and Living God seated in power and glory high upon His mighty Judgment Throne. And in one of His hands I saw the Book all torn and frayed, unrolled like an old tattered scroll. And in the other He held a golden hourglass filled with stardust.

And from out of the midst of the Throne Room I could see vast waves of holy angels rushing forth in every direction, gathering up the hordes of lost and fallen angels who had given up their portions of grace to seek after their own glory.

And when the time came for the dragon to be loosed from his prison, I saw him rise from the gloom and ascend up to heaven.

Now the dragon was exceedingly wroth with God, and

he went in and stood ferociously before the Throne, full of envy and rage. And when he opened his mouth to roar, out belched fire and smoke like that of a giant blast furnace, engulfing the inner chamber and plunging the Sanctuary into utter darkness, insomuch that I could not see or breathe.

But immediately God formed a whirlwind with His breath and blew all the fire and smoke away. And I looked and saw that the Book had turned to ash in His hand.

And taking hold of that old dragon by his tail, He flung him down into the depths of hell and sealed up the pit for good, where he shall dwell forever and ever in eternal darkness.

TRIPLE STAR CONJUNCTION

Behold: I see a new vision rising on the horizon. And with it, the promise of a new beginning.

Looking out over the flood waters from a tiny island in the middle of nowhere, I saw a magnificent sandcastle rise up out of the sea and pierce the clouds. And being transported safely to the top of the highest watchtower, I gazed up into the heavens and to my surprise, saw three bright stars move into conjunction and fuse together as one.

Now it was twilight time when this spectacular star went over and stood fixed directly above the summit of the Holy Mountain, glowing like a burning lantern.

And there was a sensational double eclipse and the moon was partially darkened and became as blood. And the sky turned an ominous deep purple as pebble-sized hail mingled with sleet began raining down from the heavens.

And a dense fog rolled across the face of the deep, totally obliterating the tiny island.

Off in the distance I heard a loud blast like the sound of

somebody blowing a giant foghorn: Turning to see who
it might be, I saw what looked like Noah's Ark as it was
tossed about by the waves during a mighty tempest, just
like a piece of driftwood when it is caught in a whirlpool.
And being loaded down with two of every kind, was sure
to be pulled under and swallowed up by the flood.

And as the ark passed beneath the eye of the storm, I
watched as a beautiful white dove was set free from a
golden cage and went in search of dry land.   And
there appeared strange saucer-shaped objects turning like
pinwheels and spools of colored ribbon unwinding in the
sky above my head. And everywhere I looked were flying
kites and colored balloons floating through the air like giant
bubbles.

And when the white dove returned from her voyage
around the world with an olive branch in her mouth, the
fog lifted and the sky brightened. And the sea calmed and
the flood waters slowly receded. And I saw the ark come to
rest unharmed on Mount Ararat.

And behold: A new constellation formed in the zodiac in
the likeness of the Holy Family, that is, the Holy Trinity,
bringing peace, love and unity to the world.

And that wicked race of giants and all sea serpents were
wiped off the face of the earth. And above the rainbow
I saw two flying eagles carrying a banner with the words
"GLORY TO GOD" written on it.

BABY RAMS

Now in the ninth month of the Two Rams' prison term I saw two promiscuous horns sprout up out of the she-goat's forehead. And when the time came for her to be delivered, she gave birth to a pair of Baby Rams with furry little horns.

But when the she-goat suddenly died during labor, I heard one of the Baby Rams start to whine. And thinking myself to be so clever, I turned to the angel and said, "I know that the Baby Ram I hear whining for its mother must be the second ram's son because he sounds just like his father!"

But when the angel heard it he just chuckled and answered, "O Great Seer, where did you lose faith in God? For the Baby Ram which you hear is not crying for its mother as you first supposed, but for his twin brother who was born deaf and dumb."

And I looked and was shocked to see one of its horns was all twisted and bent out of shape and had completely outgrown the other.

Nonetheless, no sooner did the she-goat die when some kind and charitable members of the congregation came forward and took the Baby Rams in. And they reared them up and washed them clean of their mother's filth, surrounding them with every luxury imaginable.

And when the time came, they brought the Baby Rams before God and consecrated them with the same unholy vows that their fathers had made.

After this I saw the Giver of Life enter the dungeon where the Two Rams were both fast asleep. And it was well after midnight and the light of His glory shone all around, waking one of the rams with a sudden jolt. And silently opening the iron bars, He led the ram out past the prison guards up over the old stone wall and into safe pasture.

And he made his way up the mountain to survey the

damage and see what had become of things. But the Angel of Death was sitting on his shoulder and when he saw that the river had dried up, and what was left of the arena, and the Baby Rams rolling in the mud, he was overridden with guilt and threw himself headlong over the sea wall.

So the Baby Rams swiftly matured into feisty young bucks. But the ram with the deformed horn soon outgrew his brother. And rising up with great strength and determination, castrated him as he lay with the baby lambs. And he trounced his brother's seed into the dirt and cast him down a steep icy slope.

Now everywhere he roamed the young buck was treated like an outcast and feared by all the other bighorns. And when he learned that the older ram was still alive and lay on his death bed in prison, he bolted down the mountain at full tilt grinning.

But the glorious Giver of Life appeared to the older ram as he lay in a deep sleep and raised him up one last time. And he overtook the young buck and slaughtered him and hung his head on the wall for all to see.

NEW COVENANT

After this I saw a strong angel sitting on the crescent moon in the wee hours of the morning with a bow in his hand frowning. And he took a bolt of lightning from a passing cloud and aimed it toward the earth. And when he drew back his bow, there fell fire down from heaven and purged the earth. And many were scorched to death because of this terrible plague.

And I saw another strong angel riding round the rings of Saturn with a ball of ice in his hand. And he took the ball of ice and hurled it with all his might into the sea. And instantly the waves crystallized and froze in their places, transforming the sea into a solid sheet of ice.

And the earth was plummeted into a deep freeze. And all those hiding in the mountains and caves were buried beneath thick blankets of drifting snow.

But the unbelievers were spared and chastened with fire and ice until the seventh day. And everywhere I looked I saw nothing but frost and shivering, thirst and much misery.

And thinking that the end of the world had come, I sank to my knees and begged Almighty God for forgiveness: When I heard another mighty angel flying through the heavens with the Ten Commandments shouting, "Behold: The old laws have come to naught! Let us establish a New Covenant with the inhabitants of the earth."

And he took the stone tablets and smashed them to bits against the Altar of Sacrifice.

And yet another angel appeared ascending out of the East with a golden cup filled to the brim and overflowing. And he cried with a loud voice, "Lift up your cup and drink down the wine, blood of salvation, fruit of the vine!"

BLUSHING BRIDE

Are you there my Blushing Bride or have you lost your way? Is that you up ahead? For I do not recognize you amidst such folly. Where was it you stumbled, what caused you to sway? And where are your prophets to rekindle the flame?
The dim glow of your candle can barely be distinguished at the end of the tunnel.

You are like a ship lost at sea alone in the dark, going around in circles always missing the mark.

You were once a pretty young princess adorned with precious stones. Now you just cower in the corner like a sack of broken bones.

Lush palaces and mile long halls once opened wide to greet you. Noble kings and princes bowed their heads to meet you.

For years you endured through an incredible plight. Through tears you stood up and fought for what's right But look at you now trembling with fear. Have you no heritage, have you forgotten your name? And where are your merits, have they all disappeared?

No fancy facade can disguise your barrenness, no towering spire can overshadow your lowliness. Your walls are shaking, your foundation is cracked: Fragile as an eggshell the blocks were stacked.

With humility you rose, in vanity you'll fall. But what's you going to do when the Master calls?

And where are your apostles, have they all gone to sleep? When the wolf comes a prowling do they scatter like sheep?

GREAT PROPHET

On the day the Great Prophet was born the heavenly choirs fell silent and the sun stood still in its place. Great signs could be seen in the sky and the sound of distant thunder rumbled through the countryside.

But on the day the Great Prophet was baptized, the angels wept because they knew that soon his eyes would be opened and he would know good from evil. So a guiding spirit was sent from above to walk alongside of the Great Prophet and to pick him up whenever he fell on his way down the path of righteousness.

And in his twenty-seventh year, the Lord God drove the Great Prophet down from his sacred place high in the mountains to dwell among the people and be their leader.

Now when the Great Prophet died at a ripe old age, I saw the priests and ministers and all the elders of the church gather around to pray for his soul. But a bitter dispute erupted over who should administer last rites before committing his body to the ground.

And I heard one say, "I will do it: For he first prophesied in my church and was well received of his word."

And another said, "No, as a child he was baptized in my church and I have the records to prove it."

And still another said, "No, I will do it: For it was my church he loved best."

But when no agreement could be reached, they departed from that place and went home, each to his own house.

And when three days had passed, they reconvened to try and resolve matters and put his body to rest. And I heard them saying to one another, "Has not God brought us together because of a common cause? Yet we squabble like fools and disgrace His Holy Name. Let us instead seek divine wisdom that we may deal with this problem prudently and not stir an uproar, for by now his body stinks."

But when an agreement still could not be reached as to who should perform last rites, they again departed from that place very distraught and retired to their own homes.

So later that night one of the church elders by the name of Kelcil Crathe, whom oftentimes resorted to fasting and prayer, took two of his strongest servants and broke into the chapel where the body of the Great Prophet was being kept. And kneeling at the altar of incense, Kelcil Crathe lit a candle and asked God to intervene on their behalf.

And a mysterious voice spoke to Kelcil Crathe from out of the sanctuary saying,
"Behold Kelcil Crathe, you have found favor with God: For you have kept your solemn oath and not defiled yourself. Go and give the body of the Great Prophet a proper burial so that he may rest in peace. Go and don't be afraid: for I will be with you."

So they took the body of the Great Prophet down from the altar and sprinkled it with a mixture of lamb's blood and holy water. And they anointed him with embalming oil and wrapped him in a clean grave cloth according to custom.

And when they had sung a hymn, they carried the body of the Great Prophet off to hallowed ground and laid him in a grave that they had prepared ahead of time and covered it with dirt.

And when next morning, the priests and ministers came to the chapel to view the body of the Great Prophet and found it gone, they all began to accuse one another.

But Kelcil Crathe, remembering the words that the voice had spoken, stood up boldly and addressed the multitudes which had gathered to pay tribute to the Great Prophet and immortalize his remains: "O my brothers and sisters, are we not all fellowservants of Christ and share in the same inheritance? It is I you should be accusing. For I have heard your claims and found them to be false."

And summoning his servants to stand up and bear witness to his testimony, Kelcil Crathe continued on declaring, "It was I who broke into the chapel like a thief in the night and stole the body of our beloved prophet. For lo, an angel appeared to me in a vision and said, 'Go and give the body a proper burial.'

"But I beseech you, before you take up stones and drive me out of the chapel, at least allow me to present you with my own claim."

And when the people heard it they began to murmur among themselves and took up stones to drive him out of the chapel. And the priests and ministers were furious and took Kelcil Crathe aside and sat him down in the tribunal to discipline him saying, "Why did you do this thing, and by who's authority? Tell us now, we command you, what is your claim to the Great Prophet that you should carry his body off in the middle of night and bury it without consulting us first?"

And Kelcil Crathe answered in his defense saying, "When he was just a boy it was I who opened his eyes to the presence of the Lord and taught him his letters that he would learn to read and write and gain a better understanding of his visions."

But when they heard this they jumped up out of their seats cussing and shaking their fists in anger.

Nevertheless, Kelcil Crathe stood up courageously and continued on in the words of the Great Prophet saying, "'I only have two eyes and two ears. I cannot see what you see nor hear what you hear. But in my heart I know that my words are true and hope that through them you may more readily recognize the Hand of God at work.'

"And did he not prophesy of you well when he said: 'The monkey imitates everything the fool does and the mockingbird mimics them both.'"

But when they heard this they were cut to the heart and went out to seek counsel against him elsewhere in secret exclaiming, "Let us exhume the mortal remains of the Great Prophet and cremate them inso that we may place his ashes on the altar and end this dispute once and for all, and avoid an uprising."

So knowing that Kelcil Crathe had buried him in sacred ground, they set out with picks and shovels. And a great company followed after them. And finding the fresh unmarked grave of the Great Prophet, they took up their spades and began digging frantically.

And finding the casket lying in a vault about eight feet under, they tore off the lid with pry bars and gently unfolded the grave cloth. But when they saw that the body had been mummified and showed no signs of decay, they were horrified and retreated into the hills ripping out their hair and shrieking like madmen.

After this I saw two torch-bearing angels kneeling beside the grave of the Great Prophet lamenting. And spreading their wings across his body to cover his nakedness, they lifted him up and carried him off into heaven.

FLASHBACK

The mystic meditates lazily beneath a shady fruit tree and envisions spiritual enlightenment, his key to achieving inner peace.

Through a kaleidoscope of colors which spin before his eyes, he sees the seven riders of the rainbow in their horse-drawn chariots blaze a trail of fire across the spiritual sky. And closing his eyes, he traces their path with his finger.

Ever so gently he reaches up and plucks a virtuous fruit, careful not to disturb the serpent who lay basking in the midday sun. But Cherubim watch over the garden with their flaming swords and guide the seer on his mystical journey through the land of shadows and spiritual darkness, where evil lurks behind every hidden doorway.

So taking a bite, the Mystic's eyes open wide and he sees a fleet of wooden ships sailing smoothly across a crystal sea, like white swans gliding gracefully upon a lotus-filled pond.

He is strolling down a winding road now, through a lush rain forest covered in moss and evergreen, where primeval giants tower high above his head.

Onward through the meadows he wanders, past fountains and streams where nymphs and gnomes frolic on frosted fields and hummingbirds are busy collecting sweet nectar from a honeysuckle bush. Where the first morning dew clings softly to silk-spun webs and fuzzy caterpillars hatch into beautiful living butterflies.

It's evening now and the long tall shadows of the late afternoon slowly disappear into the fading light. The mystic rests his tired feet on an old hollow log and listens to the nightbird call.

A nightowl screeches somewhere off in the distance, wolves and coyotes bay at the full moon and the wild wind howls down the canyon:

The dragon has awakened like some legendary mythical creature in a lost and forgotten story of old. The dragon's breath closes in on the seer now, surrounding him in shroud of mist.

But through the haze he sees the golden hawk with its great wings of fire descending through the twelve solar gates. And it perches upon his outstretched hand.

So he plucks a feather from each of its wings: Now he has the magic power of Almighty God at his fingertips and he soars majestically off into the spiritual sky and up to the stars.

COSMIC PLAGUES

After this I saw another strong angel riding the waves of the ocean with a trident in his hand. And his breastplate, helmet and shield were made of giant tortoise shells and encrusted with starfish and coral.

And being driven by the fierce North Wind, he rode upon a swift-finned dolphin across the stormy sea, flanked on every side by scores of swordfish and other spear-headed marlin.

Now it was around noon and the sun shone in his face. And he took his trident, and aiming it toward the South, fired it like a harpoon and split the moon in two like a nutshell.

And I watched in astonishment as two thirds of the moon fell out of the sky and disintegrated from sight. Venus and Mars, the Morning and Evening Stars, they collided in space and exploded on impact.

And I felt the earth start to wobble and vibrate and tilt on its axis, as if at any moment it would suddenly shift positions or reverse directions and spin off into oblivion.

But this was not the end of things yet and two of the outer planets were knocked out of orbit and disappeared along with their moons behind a huge cloud of cosmic dust. And everywhere I looked fragments of burning rock, balls of black powder and chunks of melting ice came tumbling through the atmosphere, slamming into the earth at full force, one right after another.

And the rivers were turned into torrents of molten lava and broke through their mighty restraints. And mountains crumbled to the sea, taking ships and islands down with them and flattening entire coastlines.

And the flaming seas began to bulge and bubble over like hot cauldrons, spilling on to every shore. And the lakes and reservoirs were transformed into lakes of fire and burning sulfur.

And those who refused to repent and remained unfaithful were brought before the Angel of the Sea, who is Luna-Diva, and steamed alive over kettles of boiling sea water. But the rest were strung up on giant fish hooks and seared with hot irons until about the ninth hour, when I heard them plead for mercy saying, "Lord God, save us from this fiery hell!" And those who confessed of their sins were set free.

And I beheld, and lo, yet another mighty angel stood upon the sand of the sea with his feet on the earth and his head high in the heavens. And with the wind at his back everyway he turned, and a seahawk perched on his shoulder, he climbed on top of a giant seahorse and rode across the raging waters to the four corners of the world with a fish net dragging behind him.

And spreading the fish net out over the face of the deep, he gathered up the souls of all those who had perished at sea and raised them up out of the water to be judged.

And many repented of their transgressions and were pardoned. But the rest were cast into a dry desert where they are tormented by wild animals and consumed by hordes of soul-devouring demons.

And thinking that I, too, would be cast into the dry desert or even the lake of fire, hid my face in a sand dune and prayed to God for deliverance: When I heard the angel answer and say unto me, "Pick up your pen and write! For as sure as the sun will rise again tomorrow, all these things must shortly come to pass. But don't be frightened: For God has seen to it that not a hair on your head should be harmed".

GOLDEN HARP

After this I saw a beautiful white-winged angel with
flowers in her hair sitting on the steps of a fountain softly
strumming a Golden Harp. And she smiled as she sang.
And the songbirds gathered around her.

And the softness of her voice sounded sweet and lovely.
And it filled my heart with such gladness that I began to
weep tears of joy.

And she sang a song of hope and salvation, exalting God's
Kingship and Majesty in these words:
All honor and glory, power and wisdom unto God,
And unto the Lamb, peace and great blessings, faith and
thanksgiving,
who redeemed us with His precious blood,
and washed us clean from all our sins.
Praise to the Lamb whose kingdom is everlasting,
Praise to the Lamb whose truth reigns in our hearts.
Praise to the Lamb whose love light shines all around us,
Praise to the Lamb who conquers all our fears.
Praise to the Lamb who freed us from our bondage,
Praise to the Lamb who broke the ancient curse.
Praise to the Lamb whose mercy and grace endure forever,
Praise to the Lamb who wipes away our tears.

GOLDEN PALACE

As is my custom, I was burning incense by candlelight when all at once the angel appeared in a vision of glory and said, "Come with me." And taking me by the hand, he led me away from that place until we came upon a beautiful Golden Palace near a clear mountain lake.

And guarding each of its seven gates were two lion-like watchdogs made of bronze, ivory and jade, with spiked collars and sharp talon-like claws. And their eyes were like flaming coals and their tails were as serpents that do have a deadly sting.

And it was given unto me a golden brick seven inches long to measure the Golden Palace. And the Golden Palace has seven outer walls and seven inner walls which divide it into six separate mansions, each measuring twenty-one feet from floor to ceiling. Six of the outer walls measuring two hundred and ten feet in length, and the other which intersects the sixth and seventh, that is, the Northwest and Southwest gates, measuring four hundred and twenty feet.

Two of the inner walls also measuring two hundred and ten feet in length, four measuring one hundred and seventy-five feet, and the Golden Temple with its courtyard and plaza measuring forty-nine hundred square feet.

The sum total of the six mansions and their seven inner walls and seven outer walls, including the Golden Temple with its Golden Altar and rows of carved masks and figurines is fourteen thousand square feet.

And the Golden Palace is fortified with seven watchtowers, each measuring one hundred and five feet in height and twenty-eight feet around in diameter, which overlook the seven gates or points of entry where the temple dogs stand guard day and night.

And the glass dome that lightens the Golden Temple, and even the courtyard and terrace, measuring one hundred and forty feet from top to bottom, and one hundred and forty feet in diameter at the base.

And the plaza platform with its spiral staircase winding its way up to the seven watchtowers rises one hundred and seventy-five feet above the Sanctuary and is supported by seven columns and arches.

And the Golden Temple without the courtyard and plaza measuring one thousand seven hundred and sixty-four square feet. And the Golden Altar with its assortment of shiny vessels, rising seven feet above the main threshold and measuring seven hundred and thirty-five square feet.

So when I had finished measuring the Golden Palace and making all my calculations, I turned to the angel and said, "To whom does all of this belong...some rich and powerful ruler?" And the angel answered saying, "Well said: For this is the Temple of the Living God."

And when he had thus said it, he set me upon his wings and carried me off to the crystal lake and showed me my reflection in the water. And he said unto me, "What is it you see?"

And I answered and said, "My reflection: Like the sun on the mountain and the rainbow around my heart." And the angel answered and said unto me, "Well said again: For it is the window to your soul."

MYSTERIES OF THE UNIVERSE

Just as the Throne of God is the center of creation and the source of pure spiritual light, the sun is the center of the universe and the source of all life on earth. And like the seven Seraphim whose celestial voices fill the heavens with glorious music, the seven lesser stars which rule the night, reflect and magnify the solar rays as they revolve and rotate in their orbital paths around the sun.

The seven cosmic flames dance up and down like fiery wheels turning through the seven planetary gates and penetrate the deep, drawing blind matter to the surface. The smaller wheels circle the greater wheels in short cycles, while the greater wheels turn in longer durations, gyrating like fabulous fiery whirlwinds, spinning through the upper and lower reaches of space.

And like electricity that sparks molecules with positive and negative energy, and causes bolts of lightning to flash down from the heavens, gravity too, is a blind force that attracts and repels, and governs the speed and direction in which magnetically charged particles accelerate through space. Space is but the path in which these fiery-tailed serpents follow and the time it takes for them to collide and form new worlds.

The soft, cold blue glow and the warm, red radiant glow of two brilliant but distant stars smile down upon their seven sons and daughters as they gather up their reflections into one brilliant ray of light. The multi-colored ray of light then drops into the abyss like a sunbeam passing through a tiny prism and illuminates the deeper regions below.

The Spirit of the Living God are His Creative Forces continuously at work, creating and destroying, from the brightest star right down to the tiniest atom.

The Presence of the Lord is in all things great and small,

visible and invisible: It is interwoven into the very fibers of
every tapestry that Mother Nature weaves.

God is the Grand Architect who designs and oversees
every mountain that is forged and every valley that is
gorged by the Seven Builders.

God is the Great Conductor who arranges and orchestrates
every harmonious chord that is struck and every vibrant
note that is plucked by the heavenly choirs.

BLOWPIPE

After this I saw an angel, swift and mighty, streak across
the face of the sun with wings of fire on his heels and a
blowpipe in his hand.

Now to him it was given dominion over the cattle of the
earth. And he took the blowpipe and holding it up to his
mouth, blew with all his strength: And there came millions
of fiery darts down from out of the sky like hail and burned
up all the cattle.

And all the milk, butter and cheese curdled and turned
sour. And all the beef spoiled and went rotten. And many
were made sick and suffered an excruciating death. But the
pigs and chickens were not harmed.

And I saw another holy angel come down out of heaven
riding a majestic white lion with golden mane. And his
hair was like that of flaming fire. And the Milky Way
shone in his eyes.

And when they had circled the earth four times, I saw
the angel go and loosen the chains from all the murderers,
rapists and child molesters, that they should have full
reign over the earth six days to terrorize men, women and
children with great violence.

Now there were many earthquakes, cyclones and wildfires

those days. And in the violence and mayhem seventy thousand perished in the City of Angels alone.

But on the seventh day they shall again be chained up in their prison and eaten alive by serpents, scorpions, spiders and giant man-eating crabs. And some overcame their lusts and were granted crowns of gold.

And there were swarms of locusts and killer bees on the land those days and millions of acres were devastated. And the number of those killed in this plague was five hundred thousand.

And I looked up and saw a beautiful ring around the moonlight shimmering in the appearance of a circular rainbow. And the angel stood atop the Mount of Visions clothed in dazzling white raiment from head to toe saying unto me, "Be holy and righteous, and seek the Lord God each day. Trust in the Lord and never lose faith, and in His mercy, He shall deliver you in times of trouble. Yes, out of love He will deliver you and make you His poor but humble servant."

GOLDEN TREASURE

After this I came upon a tiny tidepool in the sand, and there lying in the shallow water at the bottom of the tiny tidepool was a sea shell that the tide had left behind.

So I picked up the sea shell and held it up to my hear to hear the ocean roll: But a voice spoke to me from inside the sea shell and said, "Follow the beach another mile until you come upon a nest of sea turtles, and there you will find what you are seeking."

So I did as the voice said and followed the beach until I came across a nest of baby sea turtles. And there embedded in the sand beneath a palm tree was a Golden Treasure chest covered with sea weed and barnacles.

And approaching the Golden Treasure for a closer look,
I could see that it was fastened with rusty old chains and
secured tightly with a strong lock: That no other man might
come along and carry it off for his own.

Then, as I stood wondering how I might break into the
Golden Treasure, a rushing wind swept me off my feet.
And shaking the sand from my eyes, I looked up and saw
the angel walking on the waves with a golden key in his
hand.

So quickly rising to my feet, I went and took the golden
key from the angel and inserted it into the lock: And
immediately the treasure-trove sprung open, revealing
a fortune in silver and gold, pearls, moonstones, opals,
aquamarine and many other precious gems

After this we boarded a ship that had been prepared
beforehand and sailed across the reef to the shores of an
uncharted island, surrounded by ten thousand mermaids
and waterbabies.

And when we had set foot upon the windswept sands, the
angel took me down into the tomb of the great sun king
and showed me all the marvelous sights. And when we
had passed through the burial chamber of the great sea
queen and explored all its underwater gardens and secret
passageways, we hoisted anchor and set a course for home.

And sailing on our way back home, the angel brought me
up on deck and explained how the stars make their circuits
through the constellations of the zodiac, and the sun alike.
And the way in which the whales migrate to warmer waters
in the winter and colder waters in the summer, and their
relationship to the stars and planets.

But on the midnight watch we ran into a violent
maelstrom and the ship was in peril. And menacing
thunderheads loomed on the horizon.

And it was given unto me a golden rod like a staff. And
the angel summoned me and said, "Take your divining rod

and quell the storm."

So I took the golden rod in my hands and raised it up to the blackened sky: And lo, a magnificent thunderbolt shot down out of the clouds and struck the golden staff like a lightning rod, jolting it loose from my grip and sending it clattering to the deck.

And the powerful force of the electrical current surging through my body knocked me to the deck, causing me to nearly lose consciousness.

And when the angel had again set me upon my feet, he said unto me, "Now take your golden staff and cast it into the sea: For in the days of this prophesy, when you have waxed old and weakened with age, it shall become for you a pillar of strength and a sign of your unwavering faith, in that whosoever sees you walking upright will know that you are indeed a true servant of God."

And I, Tixen, saw the True and Holy Church of God rise up like a magnificent firebird out of the ashes of the Great Tribulation and re-establish herself on the earth. And all the kingdoms and nations, both rich and poor, brought forth their glory and bowed at her feet, even those that had persecuted her.

And the True Church has no need of any altar or tabernacle, for the Throne of the Living God is the altar and tabernacle of it, and He shall forgive all.

And the True Church has no need of any prophet or minister, for the Lamb and the Dove are the prophet and minister of it, and they shall lead all into faith and righteousness.

And I, Tixen, saw all these things in the vision, and heard them, and hereby testify and swear by Him who sent His angel to show them unto me, that they are faithful and true as the Spirit guides my hand.

APOSTATIC CHURCH

And I saw a great beast rise up out of the depths of the sea, like a leopard and a dragon, with seven monstrous heads. And upon its seven heads, twenty-eight horns.

And the beast was likened unto seven smaller beasts, each having four horns upon their heads. And upon their foreheads were written the names of blasphemy.

And the beast which I saw had the power to seduce, and to deceive with its tongues, and to speak destructive lies, and to frighten men with great fear that they might bow down before the beast and worship him.

But the angel came and stood beside me, and the very ground trembled as he spoke: "Don't be deceived, nor be troubled: For in these days many false prophets and messiahs will rise up to power. And forming an unholy alliance with the beast, shall lead the flock astray.

"Therefore, beware Tixen: For many from your generation shall fall prey to this diabolical abomination thinking they are doing God a great service. But fear not, nor give up hope: For indeed God will save those who remain faithful and show mercy upon those who call upon His name."

After this the graves were opened and all those who were dead in Christ rose from their sleep. And great fear and disbelief fell upon those who beheld them saying, "How can this be? For this is not what the beast has taught us."

Chaos and confusion prevailed on the earth three days. And the dead overcame their enemies and on the third day were judged favorably for their good works and found their place with God

ORACLE OF JUDGMENT

Let it be known that at the appointed time, the angel of the Lord will visit the earth to avenge the wicked, and to vindicate the blessed and reconcile them with their God, the Great Liberator!

And he shall stand high upon a magnificent mountaintop and look down angrily upon the people. And he will strike the blade of his sword against the rocks of the mountain with all his might, violently shaking the earth to its very core.

The wicked shall flee their homes and gather by the sea by the thousands, while others go deep underground to escape God's fierce wrath in the form of the angel's mighty sword of retribution.

I am the God of thunder and lightning. Lord of the four elements and I have come with a swift and decisive sword to strike the earth and divide the nations who have fallen into apostasy.

With the artillery of ten thousand armies, I shall wage war against my enemies and punish those who have turned their backs and scorned me.

With a fierce and mighty battle cry I will descend to scatter the nations and disperse the troops assembled on all sides of me: For I am the God of thunder and lightning and no weapon formed against me can stand.

City by city I will upbraid the nations and dismantle the heirarchy of evildoers. With my Hammer of Justice I will crush the powers who have exalted themselves above me.

I will scorch my adversaries with fire and they shall know that I am the Lord of the four elements: For with these I will demolish the high places of the wicked who corrupt their followers with witchcraft and sorcery, and seduce innocent children into idolatry by encouraging them to partake in their profane and perverted practices.

So shout it from the rooftops! Proclaim it on every shore!

The Lord is coming with a heavy hand to avenge His enemies, and they shall tremble with fear under His fierce indignation, and pay ransom equal in cost only to the weight of their downtrodden souls.

Behold! I will thrust my sickle into the barren earth and smite the sea with plagues. Entire nations will be annihilated: For I am the God of thunder and lightning, Lord of the four elements, and the world will bow before me in reconciliation!

But O Lord, I will be you mouthpiece among this depraved and shipwrecked nation. I will preach vehemently against foolishness, hatred and violence, and scoff at the bribes of swindlers, condemning those who fuel the fires of injustice.

O Lord, what is this deplorable sight? This abomination which lies before me? A world governed by tyrants elected by the people to promote injustice and uphold the laws that they themselves have broken.

A world gone mad where neighbor betrays neighbor and the elders are left like beggars to wander its shabby streets. Communities torn asunder by strife and poverty, where babies are butchered before they see the light of day and little orphans are gunned down in cold blood!

A nation full of murderers is what you are! There's blood on the tracks that lead straight to your doorsteps. It's even smeared across you lips.

There's no commonwealth here. It is each to their own in this rathole! The greed and the filth and the violence has spread like an epidemic run rampant, spilling beyond its borders.

Its ports have become the habitation of pirates and a haven for scavengers, and a channel for every evil vice under the sun.

- The End -

DAVID B. HARRINGTON
E-Mail: david7945harr@yahoo.com
Portland, Oregon
(503) 238 - 2800

INNERCIRCLE PUBLISHING

Seeking Publication?

Are You Aware? Poet? Author of Metaphysical Content?

Contact InnerCircle Publishing

- Over 60 Metaphysical Titles in Print -
- World-Wide distribution via Ingram -
- Drop-Ship Abilities to any location on the planet -
- Active and Exponential Marketing for all Titles -
- World-Wide Radio Exposure -
- Automated Order Fulfillment for Customers and Book-sellers -
- Authors Retain 100% of their Rights and Net Profits -
- Sales Compensation Paid Monthly -

Are You Aware?

www.rev-press.com
www.innercirclepublishing.com

Breinigsville, PA USA
07 March 2011
257088BV00001B/42/P